KU-157-063

WITHDRAWN FROM STOCK

party party party!

641.568

LIMERICK
COUNTY LIBRARY
0053 36 222

This edition first published in Great Britain in 2006 by
Kyle Cathie Limited

ISBN 1 85626 625 3
ISBN 13-digit 978 1 85626 625 7

10 9 8 7 6 5 4 3 2

Copyright © 2005 Kyle Cathie Ltd
Photography copyright © 2005 Will Heap
Book design © 2005 Kyle Cathie Ltd

Senior editor: Helen Woodhall
Designer: Geoff Hayes
Typesetter: Mick Hodson
Stylist: Penny Markham
Home economists: Angela Boggiano and Jenny White
Production: Sha Huxtable and Alice Holloway

Colour reproduction by Scanhouse Pty Ltd
Printed and bound in China by C & C Offset Printers

With thanks and acknowlegement to all the recipe writers
whose talents have contributed to the creation of this book.

With special thanks to Linda Bain, Nicola Donovan, Amanda Fries,
Sarah Lee, Kate McBain

All rights reserved. No part of this book may be reproduced,
stored in a retrieval system or transmitted in any form or by any
means, electronic electrostatic, magnetic tape, mechanical,
photocopying, recording or otherwise without the prior
permission of the publisher.

First published in Great Britain in 2005 by Kyle Cathie Limited for
Sainsbury's Supermarkets Limited.

IMPORTANT NOTES: The recipes in this book are available
online at www.sainsburys.co.uk. All recipe timings are
approximate and intended for use as a guide. Always follow
pack instructions. When cooking raw meat and fish, cook until
piping hot with no pink colour remaining.

The eggs used in this book are medium sized. All spoon
measurements for dry ingredients are heaped. 1 teaspoon =
5ml, 1 tablespoon = 15ml. Always use either metric or imperial
measurements when following a recipe – never mix the two.

contents

it's party time!

Parties – whether a small gathering of friends on a balmy summer's evening or a big festive bash – are supposed to be fun, not just for your guests but for you, too, and the key to enjoyable, stress-free entertaining is preparation. This book is jam-packed with easy, delicious recipes many of which can be prepared in advance, so that on the day all you have to do is pop them in the oven if you want to serve them hot, garnish and arrange them attractively – then relax and concentrate on having a good time.

In order to plan, you need to be clear what sort of party you are giving. How many people are going to be there and for how long? If it is a drinks party and you are expecting everyone to go home after a couple of hours, a few canapés (about 7-10 bite-sized pieces per person) are all you need. If you want everyone to be drinking your health in champagne at midnight, you need to provide something more substantial. Even so, it should be manageable finger food – the sort of thing that is easy to eat when you are standing up with a glass in one hand.

Delight your guests with a variety of hot and cold food. Chicory Leaves with Brie, Honey and Grapes (page 38) are delicious and unusual, but they'll be appreciated all the more if you mix 'n' match them with crunchy fresh vegetables served with Barbecue Dip (page 18) and piping hot Stuffed Mushrooms (page 42). If you aren't giving everyone plates and cutlery, make sure you have plenty of paper napkins so that they can enjoy hot food while it is still hot and wipe sticky fingers afterwards.

If your party is going to last all evening, don't put all the hot food out at once. Prepare oven-baked dishes like Curried Turkey Samosas (page 60) or Filo Parcels (page 64) in advance, cook half of them in time for the start of the party, and pop the rest into the oven an hour or two later when plates are beginning to empty. That way late arrivals will still have deliciously fresh food, and any uncooked leftovers can be frozen – ready for the next celebration!

Make sure that you have plenty of glasses in case people want to switch from wine or punch to something 'soft'.

Dips

These are an easy way to provide variety and, if you wish, to enhance a party's theme. Offer tortilla chips with Mexican-inspired Tomato Salsa (page 14) and Guacamole (page 16) for a true taste of 'South of the Border', go Indian with mini-poppadoms or strips of naan bread to accompany Cucumber and Yoghurt Dip (page 21) or the Dipping Naan Platter (page 26); or serve crunchy raw carrot, celery and peppers with the Mediterranean Tapenade (page 24) and Aubergine Caviar (page 32). Individual serving suggestions are given with

the recipes, but don't be afraid to experiment. Mini oatcakes, heart-shaped or round pieces of toast, mini blinis or small squares of pumpernickel bread, lightly steamed asparagus spears or wedges of cucumber and cocktail sausages all make excellent 'dippers'.

Rather than serving the dips and dippers separately, you can make them into pretty canapés by heaping a generous teaspoonful of dip on top of your chosen bite-sized base – which again can be anything from a prawn cracker to a chicory leaf. Decorate the canapés with attractive herbs – dill and fennel have pretty feathery leaves and go particularly well with fish – or sprinkle a little red paprika on top of guacamole for eye-catching colour contrast.

Most of the dips in this book can be made well in advance and frozen until needed, although anything with a crunchy texture (such as the Sesame Yogurt Dip on page 21 or Spiced Pea Dip on page 30) is best made on the day. Avocado tends to lose its lovely green colour if you prepare it more than a couple of hours in advance, but Guacamole freezes well, and you can help avoid the discoloration by sprinkling the top of the dish with lemon juice (which gives a little extra bite, too).

Assembling canapés also needs to be done pretty close to the last minute or crispy bases such as toast or crackers tend to go soggy.

Finger food

This can be as adventurous as you are. You'll see that we've suggested variations for lots of the recipes in this section, so try any of these that take your fancy and also use them as jumping-off points for your own ideas.

Remember that with all stand-up party food small is beautiful. Don't serve anything that is going to make more than two reasonably dainty bites. Use mini vol-au-vent cases for Chicken Liver Vol-au-vents (page 48) and your smallest muffin tins for Mini Smoked Salmon Muffins (page 55). If you don't own small muffin tins, use normal-sized ones, cooking for a few minutes longer to make sure the muffins are 'done' all the way through and cut them into neat halves or even quarters. When serving nibbles on sticks, as with Devils on Horseback (page 40) or Satay with Peanut Sauce (page 66), don't put more than three or four bits on each cocktail stick.

For Brioche-style Pizza (page 46), slice the brioche into small squares; if you are going oriental with Steamed Won Tons with Prawns and Chicken (page 56), don't overfill the wrappers. If you do, you run the risk of your luscious filling pouring over someone's party frocks or - worse still - your carpet.

Make food fun

Getting everyone to help themselves from a big platter in the centre of the table is an easy way to serve a lot of people quickly. You can do this with any of the dishes in this book, particularly the heartier ones such as Beef Chilli Nachos (see page 70). Our variation on the Swiss classic, Quick Cheese Fondue (page 69), is a fantastic ice-breaker if your guests don't know each other very well. Provide lots of small chunks of bread, give everyone a fondue fork and leave them to it - almost everyone will lose a piece of bread in the first few attempts and have to pay a forfeit!

Sweet treats

Just as with a larger meal, a little something sweet can be a memorable way to round off your party offerings. Our deliciously simple Stuffed Apricots (page 104) and Mango and Passion Fruit Bruschetta (page 112) are tingling palate-cleansers; Deluxe Florentines (page 114) and Lemon and Pistachio Biscotti (page 118) are a treat with the coffee; and Chocolate Truffles (page 110) and minty Chocolate Choux Buns (page 116) are pure decadence. The choice is yours!

Drinks

Whether you're aiming for cocktail-party sophistication, zingy summer fizz or warming winter cups, the ideas starting on page 70 are guaranteed to make your party go with a bang. Our chic Cosmopolitan (page 90) and cool Cuba Libre (page 92) are classics, while Pineapple Marjoram Cocktail (page 94) and Melon and Champagne Explosion (page 96) will have your guests begging you for the recipe. Alcohol-free cocktails can be just as exciting – try our scrummy Apricot Cooler (page 80) or sparkling Apple Fizz (page 82) and pep them up with Floral Ice Cubes (page 76). When the nights draw in, close the curtains, light the fire and settle down with Mulled Wine (page 88) or Christmas Party Punch (page 99).

HOW TO USE THIS BOOK: We've divided the recipes into Dips, Finger Food, Drinks and Sweet Treats, but you'll probably want to choose whatever appeals to you from each chapter. There's everything you need to make your party go with a swing!

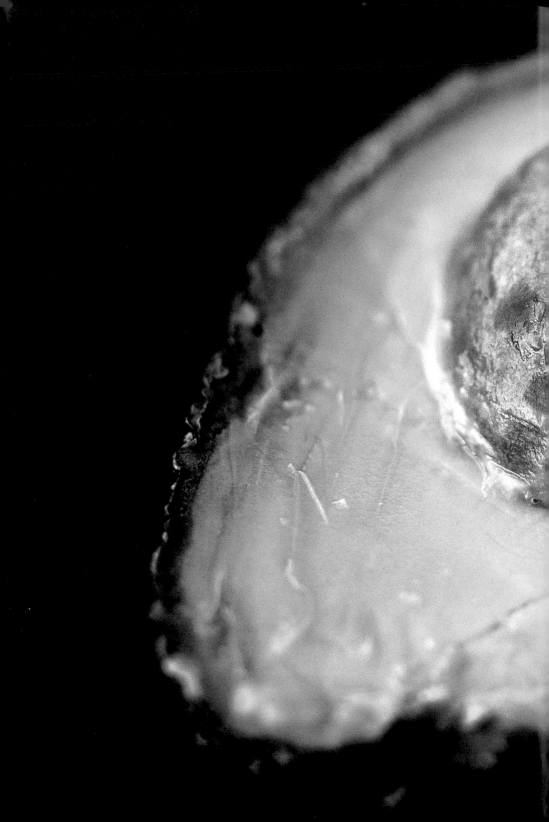

dips

fresh tomato salsa

A fantastic dip or a colourful, sauce to serve with grilled meat or fish.

prep time	serves 10	per serving	per serving
15 mins	serves 10	100 cals	8g fat

4 large tomatoes
2 spring onions
1 tablespoon white wine vinegar
3 tablespoons extra-virgin olive oil
1 teaspoon caster sugar
1 tablespoon fresh chopped herbs such as
   basil, mint or coriander
salt and freshly ground black pepper

Halve and deseed the tomatoes, and cut into rough dice. Slice the spring onions very finely and mix with the tomatoes, vinegar, oil, sugar and herbs. Season to taste with salt and pepper.

Chill until required. Serve with tortilla chips.

COOK'S TIP
Replace the tomatoes with mango or pineapple if you want a sweeter salsa.

Variation
Chargrilled Sweetcorn Salsa
Soak 6 tablespoons of black beans overnight, then drain and cook in salted water on a medium simmer for about 30 minutes. Chargrill 2 corn cobs until tender but not burnt. Scrape off the kernels and add to one quantity of the tomato salsa with the black beans and 1 chopped, roasted pepper.

guacamole

Serve guacamole with crunchy tortilla chips to add a Mexican flavour to your evening.

prep time	serves 6	per serving	per serving
15 mins		180 cals	19g fat

2 ripe avocados
125g (4oz) oil-soaked sun-dried tomatoes, drained and chopped
1 clove garlic
1/2 teaspoon ground coriander
1-2 tablespoons lime or lemon juice
1 tablespoon fresh chopped coriander
salt and freshly ground black pepper

Halve, stone and peel the avocados. Put the avocado, tomatoes, garlic and ground coriander into a food processor. Using the pulse button, whizz the ingredients together until the avocados are well chopped but not smooth.

Add the lemon juice to taste and stir in the chopped coriander. Season with salt and pepper. Serve as soon as possible with tortilla chips.

Variations
To make a more chunky guacamole relish, chop the avocado into 1cm (1/2in) dice. Add 2 finely chopped shallots, 8 quartered cherry tomatoes, a large red chilli, deseeded and finely chopped, and a crushed clove of garlic. Season with a pinch of sugar, a tablespoon of olive oil and salt and pepper.

To make an avocado, anchovy and chilli dip, dice or mash 2 large avocados with a 50g (2oz) tin of anchovies, a red chilli, deseeded and chopped, and 2 tablespoons of crème fraîche. Season and serve.

To make an avocado and cheese dip, dice or mash 2 large avocados with a tablespoon of lemon juice, 2 skinned, deseeded and chopped tomatoes, 2 crushed cloves of garlic, half a grated onion and a 60g (21/2oz) packet of soft cheese. Season and serve.

crème fraîche and wholegrain mustard dip for sausages

Simple and delicious party food that is fun for all ages.

prep & cook time	serves 10	per serving	per serving
30 mins		195 cals	17g fat

200g (7oz) crème fraîche
3 teaspoons grainy Dijon mustard
40 baby Cumberland sausages

Preheat a grill to hot.

Mix together the crème fraîche and mustard.

Spread out the sausages and grill until browned and cooked through.

Serve the mustard sauce in a bowl with mini cocktail sausages on sticks.

barbecue dip (*right*)

This tangy dip has real bite – perfect with crunchy batons of raw veg.

prep time	serves 12	per serving	per serving
15 mins		129 cals	8g fat

6 spring onions
1 green pepper
250g (8oz) red Cheddar cheese
300g (10oz) natural yogurt
2 tablespoons tomato ketchup
2 tablespoons mayonnaise
1 teaspoon Worcestershire sauce
dash of Tabasco sauce
paprika or chopped chives
salt and freshly ground black pepper

Finely chop the spring onions and green pepper, discarding the core and seeds of the pepper. Grate the cheese using a fine grater.

Combine all the dip ingredients in a large bowl, adding Tabasco, salt and pepper to taste. Mix well. Spoon into a serving dish and chill.

Sprinkle with paprika or chives. Serve with a selection of savoury biscuits and raw vegetables such as red and green pepper, carrot, celery, cucumber and cauliflower florets.

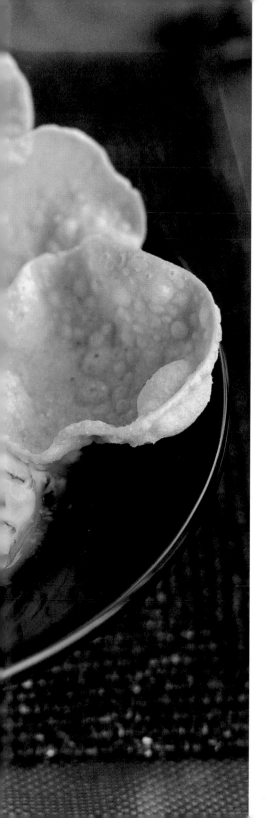

cucumber and yogurt dip

This cool dip is great with mini poppadoms to kick off a party with an Asian flavour.

prep time   serves 6   per serving   per serving

1 cucumber, halved and deseeded
1-2 teaspoons salt
300ml (1/2 pint) Greek yogurt
2 teaspoons chopped mint
pinch of cayenne pepper
freshly ground black pepper

Grate the cucumber on the coarse side of the grater. Put into a colander and sprinkle with salt. Leave to stand for 15 minutes.

Drain and dry the cucumber with absorbent kitchen paper. Mix with the yogurt and mint, and season to taste with the peppers.

Refrigerate for 30 minutes before serving.

Variation:
To make a sesame yogurt dip, mix 300ml (1/2 pint) of Greek yogurt with the same amount of mayonnaise. Add 125g (4oz) sesame seeds and 6 tablespoons of dark soy sauce. Eat the same day to make sure the sesame seeds stay crunchy.

LIMERICK
COUNTY LIBRARY
00536322

mayonnaise

A classic accompaniment to many cold dishes or as a dip for a host of vegetables. Serve it plain or in one of our tangy variations.

30 mins		404 cals	43g fat
prep time	makes 300ml	per serving	per serving

2 egg yolks
1 teaspoon prepared mustard, Dijon for
    preference
2 tablespoons white vinegar or more to taste
250ml (8fl oz) salad oil (e.g. corn or rapeseed)
salt and freshly ground black pepper

In a small bowl, whisk the egg yolks, mustard, a teaspoon of the vinegar and a little salt and pepper until slightly thick. Whisking constantly, beat in the oil drop by drop. After about 2 tablespoons of the oil have been added and the mayonnaise has started to thicken, add the oil in a thin, steady stream, beating constantly. Season to taste with more vinegar, salt and pepper .

Mayonnaise can also be prepared in an electric mixer, food processor or blender. Combine the egg yolks, mustard, a teaspoon of the vinegar and a little salt and pepper in the bowl of the machine. Turn on the machine and add the oil in a slow, steady stream.

If the finished mayonnaise is too thick, thin it with a little warm water.

COOK'S TIP
if you add the oil too quickly it will separate (curdle). Cold ingredients straight from the fridge can be difficult to emulsify so take them out of the fridge about half an hour before you're ready to make the recipe in order to bring them to room temperature.

Variations:
To make aïoli, or garlic mayonnaise, add 3 or 4 crushed cloves of garlic to the egg yolks as you start to make the mayonnaise. Add a tablespoon of parsley at the end and check for seasoning before serving as a dip for crudités.

To make seafood sauce, mix prepared mayonnaise with 4 skinned and diced tomatoes, 2 tablespoons of lemon juice, a teaspoon of Worcestershire sauce, 2 crushed cloves of garlic, 2 tablespoons of chopped parsley and 2 teaspoons of finely grated lemon zest.

tapenade

A gutsy Mediterranean treat that's great as a dip with breadsticks or crudités or spread on crunchy little toasts.

prep time   serves 4   per serving   per serving

125g (4oz) Kalamata olives
25g (1oz) capers
1 clove of garlic, crushed
3-4 anchovy fillets (optional)
5-6 tablespoons extra-virgin olive oil
freshly ground black pepper

Stone the olives and put them in a blender with the capers, garlic and anchovy fillets. Whizz together until very well chopped. With the motor running, pour the oil onto the olives in a thin steady stream until well emulsified.

Season with plenty of black pepper. You shouldn't need extra salt if using anchovy fillets.

COOK'S TIP
There are many different types of olive, so try other varieties to alter the flavour of your tapenade dramatically.

Variations:
Black Olive and Feta Pâté
Add 4 finely chopped sun-dried tomatoes, 175g (6oz) crumbled feta cheese and a teaspoon of dried oregano to the tapenade.

Tapenade, Rocket and Mushroom Toasts
For a simple starter or snack, toast diagonal slices of French bread. Top with tapenade, sautéed mushrooms and rocket leaves and serve.

dipping naan platter

A trio of tasty relishes to kick off a party with style.

prep & cook time	serves 6-8	per serving	per serving

For the Coriander Relish:
½ bunch coriander
½ medium red onion, roughly chopped
1 tomato, deseeded and peeled, roughly
  chopped
5mm (¼in) root ginger
2 green chillies, deseeded
1 teaspoon lemon juice

For the Cucumber, Onion and Tomato Relish:
½ cucumber, deseeded and sliced
1 small red onion, sliced
2 green chillies, deseeded and sliced
1 tomato, deseeded and roughly diced
juice of ½ lemon
½ teaspoon ground cumin
½ bunch coriander

For the Tomato and Cashew Chutney:
300g (10oz) tomatoes, quartered
4 cloves garlic, peeled and crushed
1 tablespoon sunflower oil
25g (1oz) cashew nuts
1 tablespoon sesame seeds
1 teaspoon cumin seeds
2 dried chillies, chopped
1 tablespoon jaggery (palm sugar) or brown
  sugar
salt

Naan breads, to serve

To make the Coriander Relish, combine all the ingredients in a food processor until you achieve a fine purée.

To make the Onion and Tomato Relish, combine all the ingredients in a bowl, then leave to stand for 30 minutes.

To make the Tomato and Cashew Chutney, fry the tomatoes and garlic briskly in the oil for 3-4 minutes until slightly softened. In a separate dry pan, fry the cashews, sesame seeds, cumin and chillies for approximately 1 minute until the sesame seeds pop. Combine with the tomatoes and garlic in a blender. Add the jaggery and salt and purée until smooth.

To serve, place the relishes and chutney in individual bowls, then serve alongside the naan bread fingers.

houmous

Everybody's favourite Middle Eastern dip - a guaranteed hit at any party.

prep time   serves 4   per serving   per serving

175g (6oz) canned chickpeas
4 tablespoons tahini
juice of 2 lemons, or to taste
4 cloves garlic, crushed
salt
2 tablespoons olive oil
1 teaspoon ground cumin
1 teaspoon ground paprika
1 tablespoon flat-leaf parsley, chopped

Put the chickpeas in a blender and process to make a thick paste.

Tasting as you go, add the tahini, lemon juice, garlic and salt, and blend very thoroughly to a light cream (you may need a little more water). To serve, spread the houmous flat on a plate, drizzle with olive oil and sprinkle with cumin, paprika and parsley.

Variation:
Red Pepper Houmous
Roast 6 red peppers, leave to cool, then peel and chop coarsely. Add to the blender with the rest of the ingredients, feeding in a few coriander and mint leaves just before the end.

spiced pea dip

A vibrant dip that will help you on your way to five a day.

15 mins prep & cook time   **serves 8**   **31 cals** per serving   **3g fat** per serving

250g (8oz) peas, cooked
2 tablespoons Greek yogurt
1 green chilli, chopped
1 large clove garlic
2 teaspoons olive oil
squeeze of lemon juice
1 tablespoon freshly chopped mint
salt and freshly ground black pepper

Purée the cooked peas with the Greek yogurt, green chilli, garlic, olive oil, lemon juice and chopped mint to form a chunky paste.
Season and serve with hot pitta bread and crudités.

COOK'S TIP
Use crème fraîche or low-fat yogurt in place of the Greek yogurt if you prefer.

Variations
Green Bean Dip
Replace the peas with a can of stringless green beans and the mint with coriander and continue as above. Sprinkle with a couple of teaspoons of cumin seeds to garnish.

Pea and Broad Bean Dip
Replace half the peas with cooked broad beans and continue as above.

aubergine caviar

A little taste of luxury from the Mediterranean.

prep & cook time · serves 8 · 103 cals per serving · 9g fat per serving

2 medium aubergines
1 slice brown bread
3 cloves garlic, crushed
juice of 1/2 lemon
2 teaspoons cumin
5 tablespoons olive oil
3 tablespoons Greek yogurt
1 bunch flat-leaf parsley, chopped
2 tablespoons black olives, pitted and
    quartered

Preheat the oven to 200°C/400°F/gas mark 6.

Prick the aubergines with a fork several times and place on a lightly oiled baking sheet. Bake for 35-40 minutes, until the skins are wrinkled and the flesh is soft.

Soak the bread in a little water and squeeze out. Set to one side. Cut the aubergines in half lengthways and use a spoon to scoop out the flesh from the skin.

In a food processor, purée the aubergine with the garlic, bread, lemon juice, cumin and olive oil until smooth and creamy.

Stir in the yogurt and mound on to a serving plate. Scatter with the parsley and black olives.

taramasalata

Classic, colourful and simple to make - another crowd-pleaser.

prep time · serves 4 · 174 cals per serving · 15g fat per serving

125g (4oz) piece of smoked cod's roe
juice of 1 lemon, or more to taste
125g (4oz) cream cheese
1/2 small onion, grated (optional)

Wash the cod's roe, leaving the skin on as it gives a stronger colour. Put it in the food processor with the lemon juice and blend to a smooth paste.

Add the cream cheese and blend only briefly so that it does not become too soft (it can turn almost liquid).

Stir in the onion, if used, and serve with pitta bread cut into triangles.

finger food

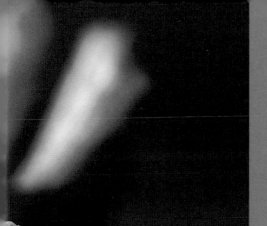

cheese twigs

These tasty treats will never go out of style.

30 mins prep & cook time

makes 40-50

15 cals per serving

1g fat per serving

125g (4oz) plain flour
pinch of salt
50g (2oz) butter or margarine
75g (3oz) Cheddar cheese, coarsely grated
1 stock cube, roughly crumbled
1 egg yolk
2½ tablespoons water

Preheat the oven to 200°C/400°F/gas mark 6.

Sift the flour and salt into a bowl. Rub in the fat until the mixture resembles breadcrumbs. Stir in the cheese and stock cube, then add the egg yolk and enough water to mix to a firm dough.

Turn onto a floured surface and knead lightly. Roll out thinly into a large square, about 5mm (¹/₄in) thick. Cut into strips 5mm (¹/₄in) wide and 7.5cm (2in) long.

Place on baking sheets and bake in the oven for 8–10 minutes, until golden.

Variation
Savoury Straws
Follow the recipe, adding a pinch of cayenne pepper to the flour and 2 teaspoons of tomato ketchup at the same time as the egg, and continue as above. Sprinkle with sesame seeds, grated Parmesan or poppy seeds before baking, if you like.

LIMERICK
COUNTY LIBRARY

chicory leaves with brie, honey and grapes

Chicory leaves make a handy scoop for a smoothly satisfying filling.

20 mins		**139** cals	**9g** fat
prep time	serves 6	per serving	per serving

2 heads chicory, leaves separated, washed
  and drained
175g (6oz) mild and creamy brie
100g (3½oz) grapes, washed and halved
2 tablespoons runny honey

Place the chicory leaves on a serving plate. Thinly slice the brie and place a slice inside each leaf. Scatter with the halved grapes and drizzle over the honey.

Serve immediately as a starter or with a selection of salads and breads as part of a meal or buffet.

Variation
Chicory with Tuna and Orange
Mix a 200g (7oz) tin of tuna in oil with the zest of 1 orange, a handful of chopped coriander leaves and a deseeded and chopped chilli. Add 3 tablespoons of ready-made lime and coriander dressing and pile into the leaves. Sprinkle with toasted pinenuts and serve.

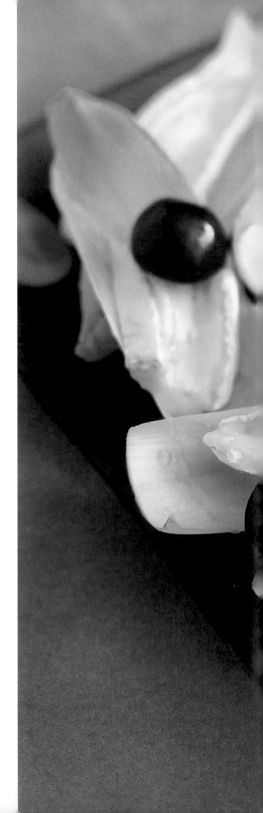

devils on horsebacks

These simple, savoury bites always go down well.

30 mins		83 cals	5g fat
prep & cook time	makes 20	per serving	per serving

25g (1oz) butter
1 medium onion, finely chopped
1 teaspoon dried sage
50g (2oz) fresh breadcrumbs
250g (8oz) ready-to-eat prunes
10 rindless streaky bacon rashers

Melt the butter in a pan, add the onion and fry gently until soft. Stir in the sage and breadcrumbs. Stuff the prunes with this mixture.

Stretch the bacon with the back of a knife, then cut each rasher in half. Wrap each prune in a piece of bacon and secure with a wooden cocktail stick. Grill for 4-5 minutes on each side until the bacon is crispy.

Variations
Replace the prunes with cocktail sausages, sliced banana or even oysters, for a really luxurious treat.

stuffed mushrooms

Who said life was too short?
These are ready in under
thirty minutes...

| prep & cook time | makes 8 | per serving | per serving |

8 large mushrooms
125g (4oz) Moroccan-style couscous
15g (¹/₂oz) butter
2 hard-boiled eggs, peeled and finely chopped
20g (³/₄oz) fresh coriander, finely chopped

Preheat the oven to 190°C/375°F/gas mark 5.

Remove the stalks from the mushrooms, finely
chop and set aside. Place the mushroom caps,
upturned, in a suitable sized tray.

Make up the couscous with the butter as per
pack instructions, then allow to cool before
folding in the hard-boiled egg and the chopped
mushroom stalks. Pile this mixture into the
mushrooms.

Place in the oven and cook for 20 minutes or
until cooked through. Sprinkle with the coriander
and serve with crisp green salad.

Variations
Use alternative flavours of couscous such as wild
mushroom and garlic or coriander and lemon.

For mini morsels that make perfect finger food,
why not try using 16 chestnut mushrooms with
the same quantity of filling?

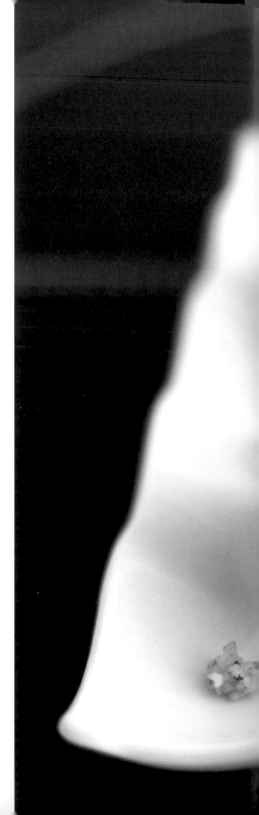

mediterranean bites

Gutsy little mouthfuls
guaranteed to wake up
your tastebuds.

30 mins		64 cals	4g fat
prep & cook time	makes 24	per serving	per serving

375g (12oz) ready-to-roll cheese pastry
150g (5oz) feta cheese, cut into 5mm (¹/₄in)
  cubes
25g (1oz) pitted black olives, quartered
1 tablespoon fresh basil leaves
2 tablespoons red pepper pesto

Preheat the oven to 200°C/400°F/gas mark 6.
Grease two bun tins.

Roll out the pastry to a thickness of 5mm (¹/₄in)
on a lightly floured surface. Cut into 7cm (2in)
squares and press gently into the bun tins, re-
rolling and repeating with any remaining pastry.

Place the feta cheese, olives and pesto in a bowl,
and combine. Divide the feta mixture evenly
between the pastry cases.

Place in the preheated oven and cook for 10-15
minutes or until the pastry is crisp and golden.
Remove from the bun tins and place on a wire
rack to cool. Garnish with basil leaves.

These bites can be eaten either hot or cold.

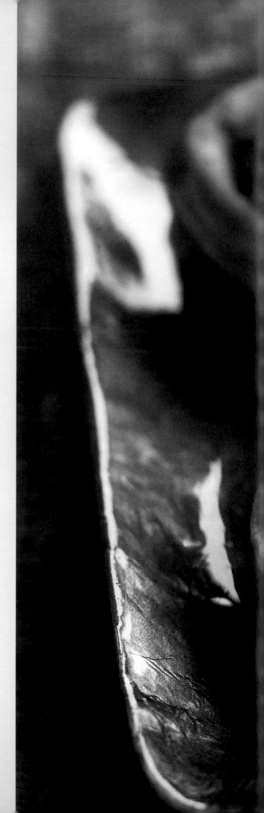

brioche-style pizza

Serve these mini pizzas as a starter or as part of a buffet.

3 hrs		272 cals	14g fat
prep & cook time	serves 8	per serving	per serving

275g (9oz) white bread flour
1½ teaspoons salt
20g (³/₄oz) fresh yeast
125ml (4fl oz) milk, lukewarm
2 eggs, beaten
3 tablespoons olive oil
flour for dusting

1 x 400g (13oz) can peeled plum tomatoes, drained
2 tablespoons tomato purée
2 garlic cloves, peeled
3 tablespoons olive oil
10g (¹/₃oz) fresh oregano, leaves removed from the stem and roughly chopped
2 teaspoons caster sugar
juice of ½ lemon
salt and pepper

125g (4oz) mascarpone
150g (5oz) baby artichoke hearts in oil
20g (³/₄oz) fresh thyme, leaves removed from the stem

First make the base. In a large bowl, combine the flour and salt and make a well in the centre. Cream together the yeast and milk, then pour into the well along with the beaten eggs.

Mix with your fingers until you achieve a very soft, sticky dough. Knead by lifting the dough in one hand and slapping against the side of the bowl. Finally, work in the oil by slapping the dough up and down with your hands. Cover and leave to rise in a warm place for approximately 1 hour.

Next make the topping. Place all the remaining ingredients in a food processor except for a tablespoon of olive oil, the mascarpone, artichoke hearts and thyme. Blend until you achieve a smooth sauce.

Knock back the risen dough, then cover and chill in the fridge for 2 hours until firm but not hard.

Preheat the oven to 200°C/400°F/gas mark 6.

Turn the dough onto a floured surface and roll out into a 30 x 20cm (11 x 8in) rectangle. Lift the dough into a suitable sized tin with a depth of 1cm (¹/₂in), and press well into the corners, squeezing out any air bubbles.

Top with the tomato sauce, then place teaspoonfuls of mascarpone liberally over the base and finish with the artichoke hearts and thyme. Place in the oven and cook for 20-25 minutes or until risen and golden brown in colour. Brush the pizza crust with the remaining olive oil and cut into squares to serve as a canapé.

chicken liver vol-au-vents

A great combination of light and airy pastry with a rich and flavoursome filling.

cook & prep time
makes 36
per serving
per serving

375g (12oz) ready-to-roll puff pastry
25g (1oz) butter
250g (8oz) chicken livers, chopped
1 onion, chopped
2 mushrooms, chopped
1 tablespoon plain flour
150ml (1/4 pint) chicken stock
1 egg, beaten
1 tablespoon grated Parmesan cheese
chopped parsley

Preheat the oven to 220°C/425°F/gas mark 7.

Roll out the pastry to a thickness of 5mm (1/4in) and cut into rounds, using a 3.5cm (11/2in) pastry cutter. Use a 2.5cm (1in) cutter to mark circles in the centre of each round, but do not cut right through the pastry. These inner circles will form the 'lids' of the vol-au-vents.

Melt the butter in a pan and fry the chicken livers gently for 3-4 minutes, until lightly browned; remove. Add the onion to the pan and cook until soft. Add the mushrooms and cook for 1-2 minutes. Stir in the flour and then the stock. Simmer, stirring for about 5 minutes. Remove from the heat and stir in the livers. Leave to cool.

Half an hour before you are ready to serve, turn the filling into a saucepan and heat gently, stirring all the while, until heated through. Remove the lids and spoon the filling into the pastry cases. Sprinkle with cheese and parsley and replace the lids. Brush with the beaten egg and bake in the preheated oven for 15 minutes, until well risen and golden.

To freeze, place the pastry cases on a tray and freeze unwrapped, until hard, then pack in a container, separating the layers. Seal and label. To freeze the filling, spoon it into a rigid container, seal, label and freeze.

To serve, thaw the filling at room temperature for 11/2 hours. Unwrap the pastry cases, brush with beaten egg and place on a baking sheet. Leave to stand for 30 minutes, then cook as above.

Variation
Mushroom, Celery and Peanut Filling
Finely chop 500g (1lb) mushrooms and 12 celery sticks and cook in butter until both are soft. Chop 150g (5oz) unsalted peanuts and add to the mixture. Stir in a small bunch of chopped parsley and 500ml (1/2 pint) white sauce. Spoon into the vol-au-vent cases and cook as above.

cheese and tomato palmiers

These simple pastry bites look really impressive and taste great.

cook & prep time	makes 20	per serving	per serving
30 mins	makes 20	59 cals	4g fat

250g (8oz) ready-to-roll puff pastry
2 tablespoons sun-dried tomato paste
50g (2oz) fresh Parmesan, grated

Preheat the oven to 200°C/400°F/gas mark 6. Lightly grease two baking trays.

Roll out the pastry on a lightly floured surface to form a 25cm (10in) square.

Spread over the tomato paste and sprinkle over the cheese.

Roll up two opposite sides to meet in the middle and press the two rolls together.

Cut slices approximately 1cm (1/2in) thick and place on the baking trays, leaving a space between each one to allow for spreading. Bake in the preheated oven for 10-12 minutes until golden, then transfer to a wire rack to cool.

Variation
Marmite Bites
Replace the sun-dried tomato paste and Parmesan with 1 tablespoon of Marmite and 1/2 teaspoon of water.

blue cheese, apple and walnut puffs

A fantastic combination of flavour: crunchy, salty and sweet all in one bite-sized package.

45 mins		116 cals	9g fat
prep & cook time	makes 20	per serving	per serving

1 pink-skinned apple, cored and thinly sliced
1 tablespoon lemon juice
300g (10oz) ready-to-roll puff pastry
40g (1^1/$_2$oz) walnut pieces
125g (4oz) Stilton
chopped chives to garnish

Preheat the oven to 200°C/400°F/gas mark 6. Grease two large baking sheets.

Toss the sliced apple in the lemon juice to prevent browning, and set aside.

Roll out the pastry on a lightly floured surface to a thickness of 5mm (^{1}/$_4$in). Using a 5cm (2in) round cutter or saucer, stamp out 20 circles, re-rolling as necessary, and place on the baking sheets.

Arrange an apple slice on top of each pastry circle and sprinkle over the walnut pieces. Crumble the Stilton cheese and sprinkle on top. Bake in the oven for 25–30 minutes until puffed and golden. Sprinkle with chopped chives and serve warm.

Variations

Make into four tartlets and serve as a starter, accompanied by a mixed leaf salad.

Sliced pear and dolcelatte cheese sprinkled with a few slivers of pecan nuts also make a delicious topping.

mini smoked salmon muffins

Smoked salmon gives a touch of luxury to bite-sized muffins.

40 mins		**86** cals	**3**g fat
cook & prep time	makes 24	per serving	per serving

200g (7oz) plain flour, sifted
100g (3½oz) polenta
2 teaspoons baking powder
2 tablespoons capers, drained and chopped
2 tablespoons flat-leaf parsley, finely chopped
200ml (7fl oz) skimmed milk
2 tablespoons olive oil
1 large egg, beaten
5 tablespoons soured cream
100g (3½oz) smoked salmon
24 small sprigs of watercress

Preheat the oven to 180°C/350°F/gas mark 4. Grease two mini muffin tins.

Place the flour, polenta, baking powder, capers, parsley, skimmed milk, olive oil and egg in a large bowl. Mix together until evenly combined.

Spoon the mixture into the mini muffin tins and bake for 20 minutes or until golden brown and well risen. Allow to cool.

When completely cool, remove from the tins and top with sour cream and strips of smoked salmon. Garnish with sprigs of watercress.

steamed won tons with prawns and chicken

Won ton skins are widely available – make the most of them in this traditional Chinese recipe.

prep & prep time | makes 8 | 42 cals per serving | 2g fat per serving

500g (1lb) peeled raw prawns, de-veined,
and chopped or minced coarsely
500g (1lb) skinned chicken breast, minced
finely
1 teaspoon salt
75g (3oz) fresh shiitake or button
mushrooms, chopped
1 teaspoon sugar
1/2 teaspoon ground white pepper
2 tablespoons light soy sauce
2 tablespoons spring onions, finely chopped
1 egg white, beaten lightly
250g (8oz) won ton skins

Put the prawns and chicken in a large glass bowl, add the salt and mix well, either by kneading with your hand or by stirring with a wooden spoon. Add all the other ingredients, except the won ton skins, and stir well into the prawn and chicken mixture.

Cover the bowl and chill for at least 30 minutes.

Cut off the four corners of the won ton skins. Put a tablespoon of the filling in the centre of the first won ton skin and gather the edges to make a bag. Lift this onto the palm of your hand, then squeeze gently in the middle as if to make a waist in the filled won ton.

Open up the bag at the top and press the filling down with a cold, wet teaspoon, so as to make the surface of the filling flat. Repeat with the remaining parcels.

Steam the won tons in a bamboo steamer for 8–10 minutes.

If you don't have a bamboo steamer, put a trivet or a soup plate upside down in the bottom of a large saucepan and fill the saucepan with hot water up to the top of the trivet or plate. Put the won tons on an oiled plate and place on top of the trivet. Bring the water to the boil, cover the saucepan and cook for 12–15 minutes.

Serve hot, accompanied by a sweet chilli sauce.

latkas with smoked salmon

Latkas are a traditional Jewish delicacy, best eaten straight away.

45 mins — prep & cook time

makes 45

43 cals — per serving

3g fat — per serving

40g (1¹/₂oz) butter
6 spring onions, finely chopped
2 tablespoons fresh thyme leaves
375g (12oz) peeled, grated potato, squeezed dry
2 eggs, beaten
75g (3oz) plain flour
3 tablespoons vegetable oil
100g (3¹/₂oz) smoked salmon
40g (1¹/₂oz) baby capers, drained
6 garlic chive stalks, cut diagonally
salt and freshly ground black pepper

Heat the butter over a moderate heat in a small saucepan. Add the spring onion and thyme leaves, and cook for 4-5 minutes, stirring occasionally. Set aside.

In a bowl, mix together the potato, eggs, flour and seasoning. Heat the vegetable oil in a large frying pan over a moderate heat and add heaped teaspoons of the potato mixture. Flatten a little and cook for 4-5 minutes on each side or until golden brown. Drain on kitchen paper. Repeat until all the mixture has been cooked.

Top the latkas with a small rosette of smoked salmon and garnish with one caper and two pieces of garlic chive. Serve at once.

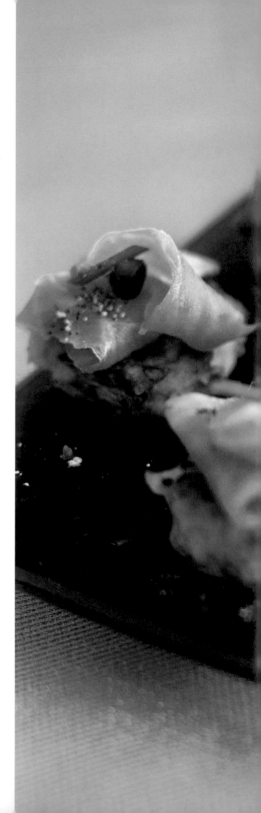

curried turkey samosas

Tuck in! These baked samosas have all the taste of the traditional deep-fried variety with less of the fat.

prep & cook time	makes 16	per serving	per serving
45 mins		82 cals	5g fat

2 tablespoons sunflower oil
450g (15oz) turkey mince
2 tablespoons medium curry paste
1 tablespoon cumin seeds
1 tablespoon tomato purée
1 onion, finely chopped
lemon juice, to taste
8 sheets filo pastry
3 tablespoons melted butter
salt and freshly ground black pepper

Preheat the oven to 220°C/425°F/gas mark 7. Grease a baking tray.

Heat the oil in a frying pan. Add the turkey mince and stir fry for 2-3 minutes.

Add the curry paste and cumin seeds and stir fry for 1 minute.

Add the remaining ingredients (except the pastry and butter) and mix well.

Cut each strip of filo pastry in half, lengthways. Brush with melted butter.

Place a spoonful of turkey mixture on the top corner of each slice and fold over so as to form a triangle. Keep folding around to use all the pastry strip.

Place on a baking tray and bake in the preheated oven for 10-15 minutes until crisp and golden.

Variation
Add a handful of frozen peas to the filling mixture.

avocado and chorizo blinis

A great taste combination – smooth, creamy avocado and spicy chorizo are just made for each other.

20 mins		77 cals	6g fat
prep & cook time	makes 16	per serving	per serving

16 cocktail blinis
75ml (3fl oz) sour cream
75g (3oz) chorizo sausage, finely sliced
2 baby avocados, halved. stone removed, peeled and sliced
1 tablespoon fresh parsley, finely chopped

Warm the blinis, either in the microwave for 1 minute or wrapped in foil in the oven for a few minutes – you want to take the chill off them, without making them hot. Arrange on a plate.

Add a teaspoon of sour cream to the top of each blini, sprinkle over some slices of chorizo and top with pieces of avocado.

Sprinkle with fresh parsley before serving.

Variation
Try this other delicous topping for blinis. Take a 200g (7oz) can of pressed cod's roe. Cut into slices and roll in sesame seeds. Fry the cod's roe in vegetable oil, mix it with crème fraîche and a few capers and use to top the blinis.

filo parcels

These tiny cheese and spinach parcels make a delicious mouthful.

1½ hrs	makes 60	60 cals	4g fat
prep & cook time	makes 60	per serving	per serving

500g (1lb) filo pastry
25g (1oz) melted butter

For the cheese filling:
175g (6oz) butter, melted
375g (12oz) feta cheese, mashed
2 eggs
2 teaspoons dried mint
freshly ground black pepper

For the spinach filling:
1kg (2lb) fresh spinach or 500g (1lb)
   frozen whole leaf spinach
125g (4oz) feta, mashed, or cottage cheese,
   well drained
a good pinch of nutmeg
2 eggs
freshly ground black pepper

Preheat the oven to 180°C/350°F/gas mark 4. Grease several baking trays.

To make the cheese filling, mix the ingredients in a bowl and set aside.

To make the spinach filling, wash the leaves, discard the stems, and cook the leaves in their own juice in a pan with the lid on until they crumple, then drain well and roughly chop. If using frozen spinach, defrost and squeeze all the water out. Mix with the rest of the ingredients and season. If using feta you may not need to add salt.

Now cut the sheets of filo into rectangular strips about 7cm (2½in) wide. Put the strips in a pile and cover with cling film to prevent them from drying out.

To make cheese parcels, brush the top strip very lightly with melted butter. Put 1 heaped teaspoon of cheese filling at one end and roll up. Turn the sides in about a third of the way to trap the filling, then continue to roll.

Repeat with more strips until all the filling has gone. Then place side by side on the baking tray and brush the tops very lightly with melted butter.

To make spinach triangles, brush a strip of filo with melted butter, put 1 heaped teaspoon of filling at one end about 2cm (3/4cm) from the edge and fold one corner up over it. Then fold again and again until the whole strip is folded into a small triangle (ensure you close any holes, as liquid from the filling can ooze out). Place close to each other on the baking tray and brush the tops lightly with melted butter.

Bake the filo parcels in the preheated oven for 30 minutes or until crisp and golden. Move the baking trays around after 15 minutes so that those underneath have a chance to get brown. Serve hot.

satay with peanut sauce

Put this in the centre of the table and let everyone dip in to their heart's content.

30 mins — prep & cook time

makes 20

54 cals — per serving

3g fat — per serving

350g (12oz) pork fillet, cut into 2cm (³/₄in) cubes
1 teaspoon chilli powder
1 tablespoon oil
1 onion, grated
1 clove garlic, crushed
2 tablespoons lemon juice
5 tablespoons water
4 tablespoons crunchy peanut butter
1 teaspoon ground cumin
1 teaspoon ground coriander
1 teaspoon salt

Preheat the grill to hot. Thread 3 or 4 pieces of pork on to one end of wooden cocktail sticks. Cook under the grill for 3-4 minutes on each side or until cooked through. Drain on kitchen paper and keep warm.

Blend the chilli powder with a little water to make a paste. Heat the oil in a pan, add the onion, garlic and chilli paste and fry gently until the onion is soft. Add the remaining ingredients, stirring well to combine. Transfer to a serving bowl.

Serve the satay with the sauce.

quick cheese fondue

French tradition says that whoever loses their bread cube in the fondue has to perform a forfeit – what form this takes is up to you!

30 mins		**269** cals	**22**g fat
prep & cook time	serves 8	per serving	per serving

300g (10oz) Gruyère cheese, grated
150g (5oz) strong Cheddar cheese, grated
200ml (7fl oz) milk
25g (1oz) butter
50ml (2fl oz) dry white wine (optional)
cubes of fresh crusty bread or croutons and
   mixed vegetable crudités to serve

Place the two cheeses in a small flameproof casserole dish (or fondue pot) with the milk and heat very gently, stirring continually until the cheese has melted (do not allow to boil).

Add the butter and wine, if using, and heat very gently. Beat thoroughly until smooth and creamy.

Serve immediately with the bread cubes or vegetable crudités such as carrot and pepper sticks.

beef chilli nachos

Spice up your evening with this hot and hearty treat.

45 mins
prep & cook time

serves 8

582 cals
per serving

18g fat
per serving

750g (1½lb) extra-lean beef mince
1kg (2lb) hot chilli con carne sauce
1 x 400g (13oz) can black-eye beans, rinsed
   and drained
400g (13oz) cool salted tortilla chips
100g (3½oz) Cheddar cheese, grated

Preheat the grill to a moderate heat.

Dry fry the beef mince for 3-4 minutes, then add the chilli sauce and cook for a further 20 minutes before adding the beans and heating through.

Transfer the crisps to 2 large ovenproof dishes and top with the beef mixture and cheese. Place under the grill and cook until the cheese is golden brown and bubbling.

chessboard sandwiches

A simple but effective way to present sandwiches.

30 mins		**74** cals	**5g** fat
prep & cook time	makes 32	per serving	per serving

50g (2oz) butter
6 tablespoons mayonnaise
3 hard-boiled eggs, finely chopped
50g (2oz) cream cheese
75g (3oz) Cheddar cheese, grated
2 tablespoons chopped chives
8 slices brown bread
8 slices white bread
salt and freshly ground black pepper

For the fillings, beat the butter with the mayonnaise and divide in half. Stir the chopped eggs into one portion and mix the cheeses and chives into the other portion. Season both with salt and pepper to taste.

Make the sandwiches using one slice of brown bread, one slice of white and one filling for each. Remove the crusts, then cut each sandwich into 4 squares.

Arrange them in two layers on a serving dish, alternating the brown and white side to create a chessboard effect.

COOK'S TIP
If you prepare these in advance, cover them tightly with cling film to prevent the bread from drying out.

drinks

floral ice cubes

Use these pretty ice cubes in summer, or in winter to cheer up the grey days.

prep time	as many as you have flowers	per serving	per serving
1 hr		0 cals	0g fat

herbs and edible flowers of your choice such as
- chive flowers
- marigolds
- nasturtium flowers
- borage flowers
- violets
- lemon thyme
- lemon-scented geraniums

Place single flowers from the herbs of your choice in the separate compartments of an ice tray.

Fill up with water and freeze.

These look pretty in a fruit cup or a cocktail, or simply in a glass of sparkling water.

Variations
Use fruit such as starfruit or spices such as star anise.

Note:
Be sure to use flowers which have been grown without the use of pesticides. Don't use plants which have grown close to roads and which may have absorbed pollution. Always wash herbs well before using.

lemonade

This home-made lemonade has a refreshingly tangy taste.

30 mins		78 cals
prep time	serves 4	per serving

4 lemons, zest and juice
150ml (1/2 pint) water
75g (3oz) caster sugar
900ml (1 1/2 pints) soda water, well chilled
1 lemon, sliced
a few sprigs of fresh mint

Remove the zest from the lemons, using either a zester or a potato peeler. If using a peeler, take care to remove only the yellow part of the skin.

Place the zest in a small saucepan, add the water and bring almost to the boil (do not allow the liquid to boil as it can become bitter).

Strain, reserving the liquid in a jug. Add the sugar to this and stir until dissolved.

Squeeze the juice from the lemons and add to the jug. Cover and refrigerate until well chilled.

Mix equal quantities of lemon cordial and soda water together and serve in a jug or individual glasses with slices of lemon and fresh mint leaves.

COOK'S TIP
Use organic, unwaxed lemons if you can. If using waxed lemons, scrub the skins first.

apricot cooler

A non-alcoholic cocktail that's a winner with all ages.

prep time   serves   per
            20   serving

1.2 litres (2 pints) orange juice
2 x 400g (13oz) cans apricot halves
ice cubes
1 litre (1³/₄ pints) lemonade
1 orange, thinly sliced

Place half the orange juice and apricots (with their juice), in an electric blender or food processor. Blend on maximum speed for 1 minute. Repeat with the remaining orange juice and apricots. Pour into 2 jugs and add the ice cubes.

Just before serving, pour over the lemonade. Top with orange slices.

Variation
Replace the apricot halves with other soft fruit such as kiwi fruit, peaches (tinned or fresh), mango etc. Add sugar or honey to taste. For an alcoholic alternative, add a dash of vodka, peach schnapps, or white rum.

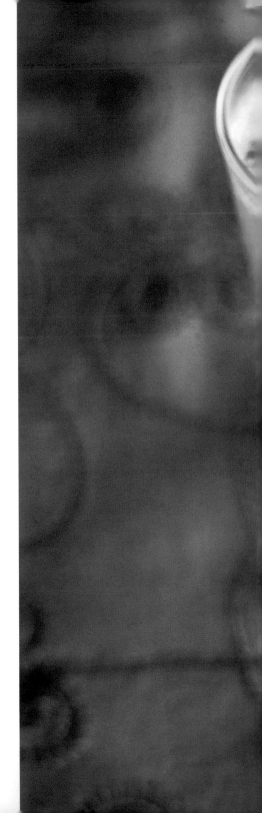

apple fizz

A fizzy drink that's bursting with goodness.

prep time   serves 6   per serving

600ml (1 pint) pure apple juice
350ml (12fl oz) carbonated mineral water
1 red dessert apple, cored and sliced
mint sprigs to decorate (optional)

Place the apple juice in a jug and add the mineral water.

Divide the apple slices between 6 glasses, pour in the fizzy apple and decorate with mint sprigs if desired.

Variations
For Apple and Blackberry Fizz, use apple and strawberry juice in place of ordinary apple juice.

For Apple and Ginger Fizz use ginger ale instead of the carbonated mineral water.

hot gingery sherbet

This warming sherbet doubles as a snack. In Java, it is often sold at the roadside along with other street food.

prep & cook time   serves 4   per serving

1.2 litres (2 pints) water
10cm (4in) piece fresh ginger, peeled and chopped
4 tablespoons granulated or demerara sugar
50g (2oz) unsalted peanuts
seeds of 1 pomegranate
2 slices white bread, cut into small cubes
2 tablespoons lemon juice (optional)

Put the water, ginger and sugar in a saucepan, bring to the boil, and simmer for 8-10 minutes, stirring occasionally to dissolve the sugar.

At the same time, but in another saucepan, boil the peanuts for 10-12 minutes until soft, then drain in a colander.

Strain the sweet gingery liquid through a fine sieve into another saucepan.

Bring back to the boil, add the cooked peanuts, simmer for 2 minutes and add the rest of the ingredients.

Take the saucepan off the heat, give the contents a stir and serve the sherbet hot or warm in a glass, with a small, long-handled spoon to scoop up the bits.

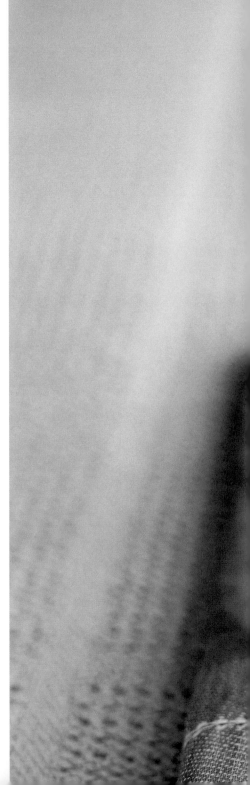

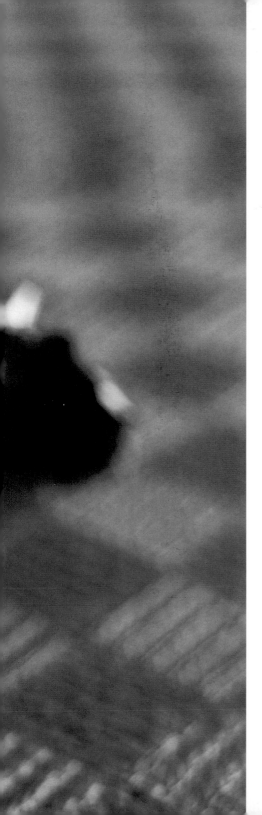

fruity rosé iced tea

A grown-up iced tea that's perfect for a hot summer's evening.

prep & cook time   serves 6   per serving

4 blackcurrant tea bags
75g (3oz) caster sugar
600ml (1 pint) Merlot rosé wine, chilled
ice cubes
10g (1/3oz) fresh mint leaves
fresh blueberries
fresh raspberries

Place the tea bags and sugar in a heatproof jug, pour in 500ml (18fl oz) boiling water and leave to infuse for approximately 5 minutes before removing the tea bags.

Allow to cool, then combine with the rosé wine.

Finish with ice cubes, mint, blueberries and raspberries.

mulled wine

A deliciously warming cup for a cold winter's evening.

prep &   serves 6   per
cook time   serving

300ml (¹/₂ pint) water
175g (6oz) sugar
2 small organic unwaxed lemons
4 cloves
1 bottle red wine
¹/₂ bottle port
pinch of mixed spice
1 cinnamon stick
a little grated nutmeg

Place the water and sugar in a large pan and heat gently, stirring, until dissolved.

Carefully pare the zest from one of the lemons. Cut away the white pith and discard. Push the cloves into the lemon flesh and add to the pan. Pour over the red wine and port and stir well. Add the mixed spice and cinnamon stick.

Bring slowly to the boil, then remove immediately from the heat. Slice the second lemon into thin slices and float on top. Sprinkle with grated nutmeg and serve.

Variation
Fruity Mulled Wine
Replace the port with a mixture of cranberry juice and orange juice. Replace the lemon zest with orange zest and serve in glasses into which you have placed a mixture of orange and apple, cut into bite-sized pieces.

cosmopolitan *(right)*

The height of sophistication.

prep time   serves 1   per serving

2 measures vodka
1 measure Triple Sec
1/2 measure lemon juice
1 measure cranberry juice
1 lime

Fill a mixing glass with ice and add all of the ingredients. Stir and then strain the contents into a cocktail glass. Garnish with a lime wedge on the rim of the glass.

Note:
1 measure is equal to 25ml (1fl oz). To make more than one cocktail, simply multiply the measures, keeping the proportions the same.

rude cosmopolitan

Shaken or stirred, you decide.

prep time   serves 1   per serving

ice cubes
2 measures tequila
1 measure orange liqueur
1 measure cranberry juice
juice of 1/2 lime
1 orange

Half-fill a cocktail shaker with ice cubes. Add all the ingredients, except the orange.

Shake or stir to combine, then strain into a chilled Martini glass.

With a vegetable peeler, carefully peel the orange as you would an apple, to create a long, thin twist of orange zest. Place in the glass and serve.

mojito

Watch out! This refreshing cocktail packs a real punch.

prep time   serves 1   per serving

6 small mint sprigs
2 tablespoons sugar syrup
1/2 measure freshly squeezed lime juice
crushed ice
1 measure white rum
12 dashes Angostura Bitters (optional)
2 measures soda water

Mix the mint in jug with sugar and lime juice. Fill the jug with crushed ice.

Add the rum and the Angostura Bitters, then top up with the soda water and stir.

cuba libre *(right)*

Another cool cocktail from the balmy shores of Cuba.

prep time   serves 1   per serving

ice
1 measure rum
4 measures cola
1/2 measure freshly squeezed lime juice
lime wedges to serve

Fill a pitcher one third full of ice, add a generous measure of rum and top up with cola and lime juice to taste.

Take a fresh wedge of lime and drop it in the drink as garnish. Stir and serve.

gin and elderflower cooler *(right)*

A sparkling drink, perfect for special occasions.

| prep time | serves 1 | per serving |

4 wedges lime
6 mint leaves
ice cubes
2 measures gin
1 tablespoon elderflower cordial
soda, lemonade or Champagne
1 sprig mint to decorate

Squeeze the juice from the lime wedges into a highball glass. Add the lime wedges and mint and stir.

Fill the glass with ice cubes and pour in the gin and elderflower cordial.

Top up with your chosen fizz.

Serve decorated with the mint sprig.

pineapple marjoram cocktail

Marjoram adds a fresh green note to this fruity cocktail.

| prep time | serves 4 | per serving |

2 tablespoons fresh marjoram, chopped
600ml (1 pint) pineapple juice
300ml (1/2 pint) sparkling mineral water
a dash or two of Angostura bitters
a measure of vodka per person (optional)
4 marjoram flowers (optional)

Stir the chopped marjoram into the pineapple juice and chill for several hours.

When ready to serve, strain and stir in the mineral water.

Add a dash of Angostura Bitters.

Serve each helping with a measure of vodka if desired, a couple of floral ice cubes and a marjoram flower floating on the top.

melon and champagne explosion (*right*)

This extra-special cocktail is a taste explosion in a glass.

prep time   serves 10   per serving

juice 1 lemon, strained
25g (1oz) desiccated coconut
200ml (7fl oz) melon liqueur
200ml (7fl oz) coconut liqueur
750ml (1¼ pints) pineapple and coconut juice drink, chilled
750ml (1¼ pint) bottle Champagne or cava, chilled

Take 10 champagne flutes and dip into the lemon juice followed by the dessicated coconut.

In a jug combine together the melon liqueur, coconut liqueur, pineapple and coconut juice drink and Champagne.

Pour into the prepared Champagne glasses and serve.

sweet cider cup

Make a big bowl of this refreshing punch – people are bound to come back for more!

prep time   serves 25   per serving

2.25 litres (4 pints) medium sweet cider
300ml (½ pint) undiluted orange squash
150ml (¼ pint) sweet sherry, optional
1 red dessert apple
1.2 litres (2 pints) soda water
ice cubes

Place the cider, squash and sherry, if using, in a punch bowl. Slice the apple thinly, discarding the core, and add to the bowl.

Just before serving, add the soda water and ice cubes.

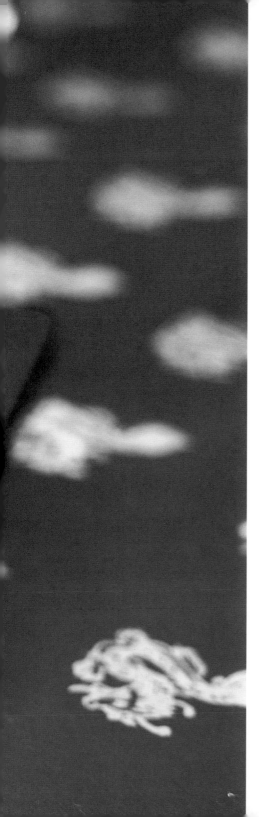

christmas party punch

A spicy punch that's perfect for the festive season.

10 mins — prep time

serves 8

101 cals — per serving

2 oranges, one sliced
cloves
300ml (¹/₂ pint) red grape juice
300ml (¹/₂ pint) apple juice
450ml (³/₄ pint) red wine
2 tablespoons clear honey
¹/₂ tablespoon ground nutmeg
1 cinnamon stick
1 apple, sliced

Stud the whole orange with the cloves. Place in a saucepan and heat with the grape juice, apple juice, red wine, honey and spices, simmering gently for 2 minutes.

Allow to stand for 5 minutes and then strain.

Add the sliced apple and orange. Serve hot.

cranberry and orange punch

A refreshingly fruity punch that's a real crowd-pleaser.

prep time   serves 6   per serving

10-12 ice cubes
600ml (1 pint) cranberry juice
300ml (1/2 pint) freshly squeezed orange juice
300ml (1/2 pint) Pimms or cider
600ml (1 pint) lemonade
1 lime
few fresh mint leaves
fresh fruit to decorate

In a food processor or liquidiser crush the ice using a pulse motion and place in the bottom of a large bowl. Pour in the liquids, mixing well.

Cut the lime into thin slices and add to the bowl. Finely chop the fresh mint and stir in.

Decorate the bowl with floating pieces of interestingly shaped fruits, such as star fruit and physalis, or alternatively thread pieces onto short wooden skewers to decorate individual glasses.

sweet
treats

stuffed apricots

Beautifully fresh, colourful and luscious, these are a real treat.

prep time   makes 12   per serving   per serving

125g (4oz) full-fat cream cheese
3 tablespoons crème fraîche
2 teaspoons lemon zest
500g (1lb) fresh apricots, stoned and halved
20g (³/₄oz) pistachio nuts, chopped

Mix the cream cheese, crème fraîche and lemon zest together, then spoon into a piping bag fitted with a star or plain nozzle.

Pipe onto the fresh apricot halves. Sprinkle over the pistachio nuts to decorate.

Variation
Replace the fresh apricots with 250g (8oz) of dried ready-to-eat apricots

almond sweets

The sweetness of dried fruit makes these dainty little treats extra delicious.

20 mins		22 cals	1g fat
prep time	makes 30	per serving	per serving

75g (3oz) stoned dates
75g (3oz) dried apricots
50g (2oz) seedless raisins
2 tablespoons pure apple juice
50g (2oz) almonds, chopped and browned

Place the dates, apricots, raisins and apple juice in a food processor or blender and work together until smooth, scraping down the sides as necessary.

Form the mixture into balls the size of a cherry, then roll them in the almonds until completely coated.

Variation
Vary the coating: try toasted sesame seeds, desiccated coconut or grated carob.

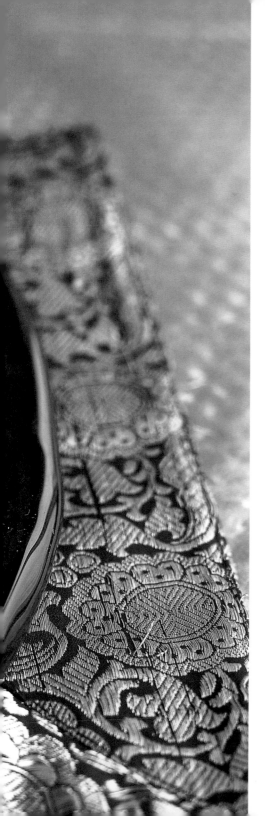

chocolate marzipan dates

Great with coffee to round off a special meal.

| 30 mins prep time | makes 12 | 254 cals per serving | 12g fat per serving |

175g (6oz) fresh dates
50-75g (2-3oz) marzipan
75g (3oz) plain chocolate, melted
25g (1oz) roasted hazelnuts, chopped

Pit the dates by scoring one side of the date and stuff with the marzipan.

Dip the dates in the chocolate and roll in the hazelnuts. Place on a piece of greaseproof paper and chill in a refrigerator until set.

COOK'S TIP
Use the best quality chocolate you can - at least 70 per cent cocoa solids if possible.

Variation
Replace the fresh dates with dried dates or apricots.

chocolate truffles

Truffles make a great present – if you can resist them yourself!

| prep & cook time | makes 20 | per serving | per serving |
| 1 hr | | 63 cals | 4g fat |

175g (6oz) plain chocolate
1 egg yolk
25g (1oz) butter
1 teaspoon coffee essence
1 tablespoon cocoa

Melt the chocolate in a bowl over a pan of hot water. Add the egg yolk, butter and coffee essence and leave in a cool place for 30-40 minutes until set.

Mould into small egg shapes with your fingers and roll in the cocoa to coat evenly.

mango and passion fruit bruschetta

Crispy ciabatta and sweet mango make a delicious combination.

prep & cook time **20 mins** · makes **24** · per slice **47 cals** · per slice **0.4g fat**

1 ciabatta loaf
2 tablespoons icing sugar
2 mangoes, peeled and cut into
   5mm (¼in) dice
2 tablespoon clear honey
1 passion fruit, seeds removed
20g (¾oz) mint, finely chopped

Preheat the grill to a high heat.

Cut the ciabatta loaf into 24 slices, then dust with the icing sugar and flash under the grill until the sugar has dissolved.

Meanwhile, place the mango and honey together in a pan and cook for 2-3 minutes, then allow to cool.

Top the bruschetta slices with the mango, then spoon over the passion fruit seeds and the mint. Serve immediately.

deluxe florentines

These delicate fruit and nut biscuits are perfect served with tea or coffee.

prep & cook time | makes 16 | 133 cals per serving | 8g fat per serving

50g (2oz) flaked almonds, roughly chopped
25g (1oz) hazelnuts, roughly chopped
25g (1oz) mixed peel, chopped
50g (2oz) glacé cherries, roughly chopped
50g (2oz) seedless raisins
75g (3oz) butter
75g (3oz) soft light brown sugar
75g (3oz) plain chocolate, melted
75g (3oz) white chocolate, melted

Preheat the oven to 180°C/350°F/gas mark 4. Line a baking tray with non-stick paper.

Mix together the nuts, peel, cherries and raisins.

Melt the butter in a saucepan, stir in the sugar and heat gently, stirring until the sugar has dissolved. Continue to heat until the mixture just starts to bubble.

Remove the pan from the heat and add the fruit and nuts. Stir well.

Place spoonfuls of the mixture onto the prepared baking tray, leaving sufficient space between each for spreading.

Bake in batches in the preheated oven for 10-12 minutes until golden brown.

As soon as the tray is removed from the oven, use a knife to tidy any uneven edges, making a neat round shape. Allow to cool a little. When firm, place on a cooling rack until cold.

Use the melted chocolate to coat the flat side of the florentines, using plain chocolate on half the florentines and white chocolate on the others. Using a fork, draw wavy lines on the chocolate. Leave until set.

chocolate choux buns

A simple and delicious mint chocolate sauce tops off these light and airy choux buns.

prep & cook time	makes 20	per serving	per serving
1 hr		90 cals	6g fat

100g (3¹/₂oz) butter or margarine
300ml (¹/₂ pint) water
125g (4oz) plain flour, sifted
4 eggs, beaten
250ml (8fl oz) double cream, whipped
15 wafer-thin chocolate mints
4 tablespoons single cream

Preheat the oven to 220°C/425°F/gas mark 7. Sprinkle two baking trays with water to dampen.

Melt the butter or margarine in a small pan, add the water and bring to the boil. Add the flour all at once and beat until the mixture leaves the sides of the pan. Cool, then add the eggs a little at a time, beating vigorously.

Place heaped tablespoons of the choux pastry well apart on the dampened baking sheets. Bake in the preheated oven for 10 minutes.

Lower the temperature to 190°C/375°/gas mark 5, and bake for 20-25 minutes, until crisp and golden brown. Make a slit in the side of each bun to allow the steam to escape and cool on a wire rack.

Using a piping bag fitted with a 1cm (¹/₂in) fluted nozzle, pipe whipped cream into each choux bun.

To make the sauce, place the chocolate mints and single cream in a small heatproof bowl over a pan of simmering water. When the chocolate has melted, stir until the sauce is smooth. Spoon a little sauce over each bun and leave to set.

lemon and pistachio biscotti

These crisp Italian biscuits are perfect with coffee or ice cream.

| prep & cook time | makes 16 | 158 cals per serving | 6g fat per serving |

250g (8oz) plain flour
1 teaspoon baking powder
175g (6oz) caster sugar
pinch of salt
2 eggs
grated zest of 3 lemons
1 tablespoon lemon juice
100g (3¹/₂oz) blanched almonds, toasted and chopped
50g (2oz) pistachios, chopped

Preheat the oven to 180°C/350°F/gas mark 4.

Place all the ingredients in a mixing bowl and mix to form a firm dough. Roll into a ball, cut in half and roll each portion into a sausage shape before placing on a lightly floured baking sheet.

Place in the preheated oven for 10 minutes. Remove from the oven, cool for 5 minutes, then use a serrated knife to cut into diagonal slices, 1cm (¹/₂in) thick.

Arrange the slices on the baking tray and return to the oven for a further 15 minutes to turn slightly golden. Transfer to a wire rack to cool and crisp up.

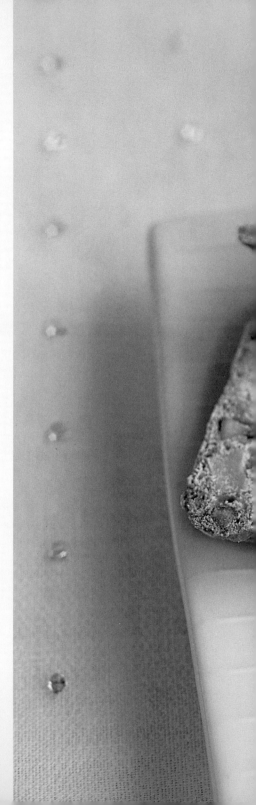

sticky soy and honey walnuts

These delicious sweet and savoury toasted nuts are the perfect treat to round off an evening.

20 mins		155 cals	14g fat
prep & cook time	serves 8-10	per serving	per serving

200g (7oz) walnut halves
4 tablespoons light soy sauce
2 tablespoons clear honey

Place a frying pan over a moderate heat. When hot, add the walnuts and toast for 2–3 minutes until lightly browned.

Stir in the soy sauce and honey and cook for a further few seconds, stirring continually until the liquid has evaporated and the nuts are evenly coated.

Spread out on a plate to cool.

filo mincemeat parcels

Delicious as sweet finger food or topped with vanilla ice cream as a dessert.

30 mins		230 cals	4g fat
prep & cook time	makes 8	per serving	per serving

200g (7oz) filo pastry
400g (13oz) mincemeat
grated rind of 1 orange
20g (³/₄oz) butter, melted
1 tablespoon icing sugar

Preheat the oven to 190°C/375°F/gas mark 5.

Trim the pastry sheets and cut into 24 squares measuring approximately 15 x 15cm (6 x 6in).

Place 3 filo pastry squares on top of each other at a slight angle to form a 12-pointed star.

Place a heaped tablespoon of the mincemeat in the centre and add a little grated orange zest. Carefully pick up the pastry corners to enclose the filling and press together to form a parcel.

Repeat with the remaining pastry and mincemeat to make 8 parcels. Arrange on a baking tray and lightly brush with melted butter.

Place in the preheated oven and cook for 10-15 minutes until crisp and golden.

Dust with icing sugar. Serve hot or cold.

LIMERICK COUNTY LIBRARY

index